# Hauling the Tide

# Hauling the Tide

Haiku Society of America
Members' Anthology
2024

Edward Cody Huddleston
Editor

# Hauling the Tide

ISBN: 978-1-930172-25-8

Copyright © 2024 by the Haiku Society of America, Inc.

All rights revert to the authors and artist upon publication.

All prior copyrights are retained by contributors. Full rights revert to contributors upon publication in this members' anthology. The HSA retains the right to publish the work on HSA social media, with proper citation. The Haiku Society of America, its officers, and the members' anthology editor assume no responsibility for the views of any contributors whose work appears in the anthology, nor for research errors, infringement of copyright, or failure to make proper acknowledgment of previously published material.

Each poem in this anthology was chosen by the editor from a selection of unpublished haiku and senryū submitted by current members of the Haiku Society of America. Each participating member has one poem in the anthology.

Editor: Edward Cody Huddleston

Layout: Tanya McDonald

Cover artwork: TheUjulala *https://pixabay.com/users/theujulala-59978*

# Introduction

As haiku poets, our domain is that of the moment, our lives measured not by the rotations of celestial bodies but by the breaths taken by our own bodies. Eternity is forever out of reach. The haiku, the one-breath, one moment poem, embodies our lives individually and life itself, capturing its essence and conveying it with brevity and brilliance unique to the medium. If the nature of nature itself is to grow vast, cold, and dark through the inevitable expansion and entropy of the universe, let our tiny poems bring forth the brief, burning lights of our lives.

Thank you for sharing your light with me. Thank you to Bryan Rickert for entrusting this venture to me and thank you to Allyson Whipple for creating a superb editorial guide for me. A huge debt of gratitude is also owed to Tanya McDonald for formatting this anthology. Thank you all for the once-in-a-lifetime honor of curating this collection. The haiku you have entrusted to me have brought me closer to all of you and closer to myself.

Yours in poetry,
Edward Cody Huddleston

halley's comet
   the bend of light in
a bunting's indigo

     *Meredith Ackroyd*
     *Afton, Virginia*


her name is Rosa
don't underestimate her
there's power in pink

     *Elaine Parker Adams*
     *Houston, Texas*

xanthic glow
of the burning log
my dying friend

    *Mimi Ahern*
    *San Jose, California*


dandelion field
same old wish
scattered on the wind

    *Dennise Aiello*
    *Benton, Louisiana*


our love songs
early morning rain falls
on my playlist

    *Jessica Allyson*
    *Ottawa, Canada*

moving up in life—
that treehouse
i always desired

*Rupa Anand*
*New Delhi, India*

tomato slices
on a bamboo cutting board
his first apartment

*Barbara Mosbacher Anderson*
*Northfield, Minnesota*

patchwork quilt
piecing the memories
of our life together

*Cynthia Anderson*
*Yucca Valley, California*

drifting petals—
a luna moth clings
to my finger

*Jenny Ward Angyal*
*Gibsonville, North Carolina*


faded prayer flags
blown to shreds
I make tea

*Lois Anne*
*Rockland, Maine*


overgrown grasses
bend all same way, one sunset
striping every blade

*Aaron Anstett*
*Japan*

airport lounge
QR code to order
a bowl of home

*Fay Aoyagi*
*San Francisco, California*


twisted vines
grown into a cyclone fence
how children adapt

*Betty Arnold*
*Saratoga, California*


the roar
where two streams merge
bud-tipped branches

*Eric Arthen*
*Worthington, Massachusetts*

sunny noon
on the pond
branches hanging upwards

*Inas Asfari*
*Oak Creek, Wisconsin*

mockingbird
one rain drop drifts
into another

*Marilyn Ashbaugh*
*Edwardsburg, Michigan*

crisp morning air
takes a bite
out of my breath

*Kathi Ashmore*
*Janesville, Wisconsin*

blackbird song
longing for home
a riff of sky

    *Joanna Ashwell*
    *Barnard Castle, United Kingdom*


rainy day—
daffodils twirls their
sunshine skirts

    *Marcie Flinchum Atkins*
    *Fairfax, Virginia*


you are the music
I am the heartfelt lyrics
we are a love song

    *Carolyn Marie Baatz*
    *Springfield, Massachusetts*

borrowed light
a space the breadth
of a book

> *Steve Bahr*
> *Roseburg, Oregon*

crayons . . .
suddenly, the clouds
turn blue

> *Don Baird*
> *Wake Forest, North Carolina*

morning shower migrating snow geese through color

> *Chandra Bales*
> *Albuquerque, New Mexico*

the temple bell unfurling a fiddlehead fern

*Jo Balistreri*
*Waukesha, Wisconsin*

summer fires—
his ashes contained
in a pine box

*Michelle Ballou*
*Bellingham, Washington*

Super Blue Moon
cataract surgery
makes it so

*Caroline Giles Banks*
*Minneapolis, Minnesota*

a copy
of my birth certificate
paper moon

*Francine Banwarth*
*Dubuque, Iowa*


vigil candles trembling outline of lichen

*Sheila Barksdale*
*Gotherington, United Kingdom*


outlasting the cutting
mower blades
the dandelions' yellow

*Peter Barnes*
*El Cajon, California*

Swinging a golf club
There's a lot not to
Think about

> *Mike Barzacchini*
> *East Dundee, Illinois*

 

oyster brine
on my tongue's tip
a tidal moon

> *Dyana Basist*
> *Santa Cruz, California*

 

tree frog chorus drowning out interstate traffic

> *Sam Bateman*
> *Everett, Washington*

light bulb dangling
sweltering tropical night
cajoling insects

*Susan K Beard*
*Sandpoint, Idaho*




sweeping away
the cobwebs
cricket song

*Roberta Beary*
*Washington, DC*




early spring
the emergence
of yard sale signs

*Lori Becherer*
*Millstadt, Illinois*

maple buds . . .
conservation land
birding into song

*Brad Bennett*
*Arlington, Massachusetts*


yesterday's sun now snow between trees

*Bennett Berardi*
*Grass Valley, California*


early spring
a fern uncurls
its question mark

*Maxianne Berger*
*Outremont, Quebec, Canada*

the snow
moves with purpose
chairs vanishing

*Jerome Berglund*
*Minneapolis, Minnesota*


we follow seven orcas
as they surface and breathe
leaving us breathless

*John Berkley*
*Statesville, North Carolina*


blizzard outside:
first slurp of the stew
burns my lip

*Shiva Bhusal*
*Bellevue, Washington*

roadworks
a row of daffodils
defy the bulldozer

*Bisshie*
*Zürich, Switzerland*

      wind swept leaves . . .
      following the drift
      of their words

          *Elizabeth Black*
          *Haymarket, Virginia*

          last to leave
          the factory
          big cold moon

              *Shawn Blair*
              *Cohoes, New York*

dragon scales stretch
over treasured gold
—glass teapot

*Jack Blocker*
*Arlington, Virginia*


swollen fingers
tie one more forget-me-knot
baby quilt

*Shannon M. Blood*
*Olympia, Washington*


after the funeral
no one wants to leave
the kid's table

*Jacob Blumner*
*Flint, Michigan*

between
doctors appointments
a scotch and soda

*Mykel Board*
*New York, New York*

dipping quietly
my paddle parts
the clouds

*Susan Bond*
*Winnipeg, Canada*

birdwatching
the black metronome
of my cat's tail

*Miriam Borne*
*Montgomery, Alabama*

his final whimper
trying to tell me
he wanted out

*Andrea Boughton*
*Littleton, Colorado*


moon moth
among the daylilies . . .
somewhere

*brett brady*
*Haiku, Hawaii*


over the fireplace
a mounted stag
stares into the past

*Henry Brann*
*Philadelphia, Pennsylvania*

sitting with water
what will I let
me be

*Luke Brannon*
*Bothell, Washington*


returning home
wrapped in red, white and blue
empty casket

*Ashley Charlotte Brennan*
*New Orleans, Louisiana*


rinsing a scallop shell in the sea   Venus

*Chuck Brickley*
*Daly City, California*

back seat driver
the country road parting
sea oats

*Randy Brooks*
*Taylorville, Illinois*

winter cold
empty
tissue box

*S. David Broscious*
*Cincinnati, Ohio*

placing memorial flags
a frightened cat
deserts its post

*Daniel W. Brown*
*Red Hook, New York*

from the charred earth
sourwood sapling—
leaves flaming red

*LaMon Brown*
*Birmingham, Alabama*




bird, squirrel, chipmunk
tracks make a wreath
around the feeder

*Roberta Brown*
*Royal Oak, Michigan*




horizon fading
blue sky
blue sea

*B. L. Bruce*
*Corralitos, California*

racing
over the kite flyers
cloud shadows

*Chris Bruner*
*Albuquerque, New Mexico*


broken glass
I see myself
in the pieces

*Robert Bruntil*
*Bellingham, Washington*


redwood bridge
a shallow creek
divides the trail

*John Budan*
*Newberg, Oregon*

a blur of blossoms
from the plum tree
spring breeze

*Marjorie Buettner*
*Chisago City, Minnesota*

the children's prayer flags
flutter in the frosty wind
speaking in tongues

*Merle Burgess*
*Yorktown, Virginia*

he claims to know me
better than I know myself
cold front

*Alanna C. Burke*
*Santa Fe, New Mexico*

black swans
the lone cygnet
paddles the sunlight

*Marylyn Burridge*
*Albuquerque, New Mexico*

peering over
the edge of today—
moonrise

*Sondra J. Byrnes*
*Santa Fe, New Mexico*

clementines
in a glass bowl
becoming Matisse

*Claire Vogel Camargo*
*Austin, Texas*

bedtime
the feral cat watches t.v.
with my husband

*Pris Campbell*
*Lake Worth, Florida*


after surgery
moon
scar

*Joan Canby*
*Garland, Texas*


old lighthouse
sepia tones
in the foghorn

*Theresa A. Cancro*
*Wilmington, Delaware*

low
tide
sundown
kingfishers
pilfer
silhouettes

    *Matthew Caretti*
    *Pago Pago, American Samoa*


        young snail
        heading for Mt. Fuji—
        take me too

            *Teri White Carns*
            *Anchorage, Alaska*


    solar eclipse
    the totality
    of totality

        *Ken Carrier*
        *Wakefield, Massachusetts*

spring in my step
under the earth
trains rumble

*Wes Carrington*
*Fairfax, Virginia*

writing a haiku . . .
I overthink it

*R. P. Carter*
*Ancaster, Ontario, Canada*

my neighbor's black tulips
translating winter

*David Cashman*
*Providence, Rhode Island*

meteor shower
does no one
apologize anymore?

    *Erin Castaldi*
    *Mays Landing, New Jersey*

dawn star
the pencil mark
where his head was

    *Aidan Castle*
    *Tacoma, Washington*

barn spider
weaving sunlight
winter's loom

    *Anna Cates*
    *Wilmington, Ohio*

flowers bloom
flowers sleep
cycle complete

*Paul Causey*
*Saint Jo, Texas*

autumn maple;
the old dog
lifts a leg

*Joan Cheng*
*Boulder, Colorado*

last day of school
her *pretty please*
by the ice cream shop

*Antoinette Cheung*
*Vancouver, Canada*

rush hour
reading his bumper stickers
too closely

> Thomas Chockley
> Plainfield, Illinois

soup kitchen line
searching for a poem
in the wall graffiti

> Jackie Chou
> Pico Rivera, California

breathing slowly
as her life slips away
first cricket song

> Margaret Chula
> Portland, Oregon

cherry blossoms
we stitch our grief
into the quilt

*L. Teresa Church*
*Durham, North Carolina*


the cold spot
after she left

*John Paul Ciarrocchi*
*Skowhegan, Maine*


a red fox rotates
the ear of an eastern cottontail
three spruces

*Joshua St. Claire*
*York County, Pennsylvania*

the tick of the tide
moon march
teases the sun

*Gordon Clark*
*Damariscotta, Maine*

lake swim—
beneath the surface
my thoughts are louder

*Rick Clark*
*Seattle, Washington*

alone
in the hot tub
singing

*Marcyn Del Clements*
*Claremont, California*

midnight prayers
dust whittles what's left
of the barn

> *Glenn G. Coats*
> *Carolina Shores, North Carolina*

if it pleases you
go against the current
the paddle stirs the soup

> *Lee Cobert*
> *Port Townsend, Washington*

flower moon
night wind blushes
in jasmine

> *Wendy Cobourne*
> *Homestead, Florida*

just a little lost
the sound of raindrops
on my trail map

> *Stephen Colgan*
> *Oakland, California*

falling chestnuts
splash in the pond
ducks flying

> *Howard Colyer*
> *Hastings, England*

burst of yellow gold
dawn invades the world
from left field

> *Sophia Conway*
> *Vancouver Island, Canada*

OCD
diving down
another rabbit hole

*Bryan D. Cook*
*Orleans, Ontario, Canada*

autumn morning
two widowers on our street
share a walk

*Wanda Cook*
*Hadley, Massachusetts*

canal currents
the duck paddles through
a tugboat's wake

*Paul Cordeiro*
*Dartmouth, Massachusetts*

my garden
in a dewdrop
my garden

>*Sue Courtney*
>*Orewa, New Zealand*

another birthday
first green
on the willow

>*Dina E Cox*
>*Unionville, Ontario, Canada*

facing the window
my eyes
fill with snow

>*Nichael Cramer*
>*Guilford, Vermont*

edge of the surf
footprints hold the moment
for a moment

> *Tim Cremin*
> *Andover, Massachusetts*

this wound that heals slow moving clouds

> *Alvin B. Cruz*
> *Philippines*

I think
of the Sphinx
new cane

> *Daniel Shank Cruz*
> *Jersey City, New Jersey*

a Goliath frog
huge in the world
a newborn's size

*Patricia Cruzan*
*Fayetteville, Georgia*

scent of rain
as ferns unfurl
a spring breeze

*Dan Curtis*
*Victoria, Canada*

roadside crucifix
a dry leaf stops
at its foot

*Maya Daneva*
*Enschede, Netherlands*

first bloom
breaching the snow
skunk cabbage

 *Keith Davies*
 *Ware, Massachusetts*

buying 12 bagels
given the senior discount—
without my asking

 *Lew Davis*
 *Moraga, California*

singing bowls
the echo of my
birth star

 *Pat Davis*
 *Concord, New Hampshire*

meandering bees
imbibing the bottlebrush
free spirits

*Danny Daw*
*Denton, Texas*

spring river
we can't willow our way
out of this

*Cherie Hunter Day*
*Menlo Park, California*

screeching
the stone-cutter's saw
and grackles

*Nancy Taylor Day*
*Austin, Texas*

spring storm
daffodils
dancing in the wind

> *Juan Edgardo De Pascuale*
> *Gambier, Ohio*

amidst wildflowers
a molded love note
and mushrooms

> *Kathleen P. Decker*
> *Williamsburg, Virginia*

rusty oarlocks
the sound of geese rising
through fog

> *Billie Dee*
> *San Miguel, New Mexico*

barn swallow
clay and fiber
canyon adobe

*Vincent DeFatta*
*Fort Smith, Arkansas*


Eclipse Day the flutist glances up between notes

*M. R. Defibaugh*
*Chesterfield, Virginia*


thunder rumbles
she has the last word
then has it again

*Jim DeLong*
*Des Moines, Washington*

sleeping kitten
a bit larger tonight
crescent moon

*Rob DePaolo*
*Newburyport, Massachusetts*

Full moon wreathed in cloud;
Its warm glow bathing the earth
this November night.

*Robert Dewar*
*Edinburgh, Scotland*

ivory and dentin
the elephant teeth
veneered to whiteness

*Elliot Diamond*
*Philadelphia, Pennsylvania*

sirens at midnight . . .
inner city heat
lingers

*Charlotte Digregorio*
*Winnetka, Illinois*


Moab autumn
painted with light
and deep shadow

*Thomas Dodge*
*Santa Fe, New Mexico*


glowing eye peering
at deep shadows within me
I stand here exposed

*Sherri Dombrosky*
*Liberty, South Carolina*

cold wind
our old hound's
last breath

*Fred Donovan*
*Chatham, Massachusetts*


taking a bite
of my ham and swiss . . .
a tiny bee

*Janice Doppler*
*Easthampton, Massachusetts*


approaching storm
the silence of a
perched crow

*Hans C. Dringenberg*
*Kingston, Ontario, Canada*

polka dot kites
against the wind
ladybug on my thumb

*M F Drummy*
*Longmont, Colorado*

I prayed hard for spring
April snowstorms my reward
dare I hope for May?

*Aimé E Duclos*
*South Berwick, Maine*

sneezing fit
late autumn aches
in my hip

*Michael Dudley*
*Chatham, Ontario, Canada*

a lone poet
looks deeply at
a lone pine

*Flora Inez Eberhart*
*Milton, Georgia*


breath of spring
the dove chick
pips its shell

*Lynn Edge*
*Tivoli, Texas*


the last bees
in the last blossoms . . .
a bud vase will suffice

*Anna Eklund-Cheong*
*Croissy-sur-Seine, France*

ragged mom with stroller
walking along the busy road
as invisible as the Beatitudes

*Jim Ellis*
*Auburn, New York*




Los Feliz—
golden light gilds and threads
the pine needles

*Jonathan English*
*Washington, DC*




abstract wall art—
finding my way back
Dad's death day

*Robert Epstein*
*El Cerrito, California*

alone
watching the breaking waves
calming chaos

    *Robert Erlandson*
    *Birmingham, Michigan*


wormwood
the bitterness
of your tongue

    *Eavonka Ettinger*
    *Long Beach, California*


my mother's last breaths
chickadee's soft
window strikes

    *Judson Evans*
    *Holbrook, Massachusetts*

windmills
churning clouds
a lighter shade of grey

*Adele Evershed*
*Wilton, Connecticut*

artificial intelligence . . .
the heron
and its reflection

*Keith Evetts*
*Thames Ditton, United Kingdom*

song on the radio
my father's smile
ashes on the wind

*Mike Fainzilber*
*Rehovot, Israel*

camping trip
the night sky filled
with myth

*Elizabeth Fanto*
*Baltimore, Maryland*

the sky explodes
in brilliant pink
a Barbie sunrise

*Susan Farner*
*Urbana, Illinois*

afternoon twilight
I close my eyes to block out
memories

*Mark Stuart Farrar*
*Snowflake, Arizona*

squirrels' tails
like silkworms
lash naked maple

    *Frances Farrell*
    *Coon Rapids, Minnesota*


new moon
my first night
without him

    *Colleen M. Farrelly*
    *Miami, Florida*


waiting for the doctor
to call
the faucet drips

    *Jeanne Favret*
    *Albuquerque, New Mexico*

an off-key symphony
warms up
wood frogs

*Barbara Feehrer*
*Westford, Massachusetts*



a duckling drifts downstream we call him Moses

*Bruce H. Feingold*
*Berkeley, California*



the sun blinked
twilight fell all 'round
once in my life

*Andy Felong*
*Redwood City, California*

sale on his favorite cereal
ends today
MRI tomorrow

*Nancy Marie Fernandez*
*Irvine, California*



first light
a mourning dove's
hue and tone

*Thomas Festa*
*Highland, New York*



ladybug
on my fingertip . . .
please stay

*Joan Fingon*
*Ventura, California*

haiku journal
a bee lands on
*deep winter*

> *P. H. Fischer*
> *Vancouver, Canada*

a toddler
the bow in her hair bouncing
dances on the pew

> *Michael Flanagan*
> *Saint Paul, Minnesota*

lost and found—
the loud whistle
of an acorn cap

> *Denise Fontaine-Pincince*
> *Belchertown, Massachusetts*

Summer afternoon
    flirting among the roses
        two white butterflies

        *Sylvia Forges-Ryan*
        *North Haven, Connecticut*



        between the notes
        of the sparrow's song
        the sparrow's song

            *Mark Forrester*
            *Hyattsville, Maryland*



still
    long enough
to watch
      the leaf fall
    all the way
      to the
      ground

            *Robert Forsythe*
            *Annandale, Virginia*

shimmering stars
damselflies
pairing

*Jason Freeman*
*Camden, Maine*

Antebellum festival
old magnolias planted
by slave hands

*Terri L. French*
*Huntsville, Alabama*

the question
of identity . . .
the owl's answer

*Jay Friedenberg*
*Sleepy Hollow, New York*

fifty-five tabs open swivel chair

*Seth Friedman*
*Bellingham, Washington*

lawn chairs—
the going somewhere
of a passing plane

*Ben Gaa*
*St. Louis, Missouri*

solar flare
dad's long held anger
lashing out

*William Scott Galasso*
*Laguna Woods, California*

smell of mown grass
a faded bronze statue
superintends

*Michael J. Galko*
*Houston, Texas*


collecting milkweed pods
my leather oxfords
split

*Cynthia Gallaher*
*Chicago, Illinois*


an old man
indecisive at the door . . .
unisex restroom

*Al Gallia*
*Lafayette, Louisiana*

smoke
rising: a plume
      of geese
heads north

*Dianne Garcia*
*Seattle, Washington*


starry night
I put a coat
on the scarecrow

*Garry Gay*
*Santa Rosa, California*


the patience
of a grey heron
koi shimmer

*Marilyn Gehant*
*San Jose, California*

birds nesting
on budding tree branches
home again

*Nicholas Gentile*
*York, South Carolina*


petals falling in love notes of Chopin

*Lisa Gerlits*
*Silverton, Oregon*


storm's end
a straggle of wild geese
rejoining the V

*Ferris Gilli*
*Marietta, Georgia*

starting the day
with hymns of praise
rain lilies

    *Robert Gilliland*
    *Austin, Texas*


sharing music
with others
sharing music

    *Joette Giorgis*
    *Port St. Lucie, Florida*


morning prayers
for forgiveness
wild allium

    *Susan Godwin*
    *Madison, Wisconsin*

salamanders
under water
spring fever

    *Kathy Goldbach*
    *Campbell, California*




wild tigers
lead
solitary lives

    *Connie Goodman-Milone*
    *Miami, Florida*




the picket line
ants parade
with crumbs

    *LeRoy Gorman*
    *Napanee, Ontario, Canada*

autumn rain
her name
on a napkin

*Adam Graham*
*Asheville, North Carolina*


wild cherry blooms
petals fall on forest trail
my petals, your path

*JC Graham*
*Vashon, Washington*


poetry reading
the clouds don't seem as lonely
field of folding chairs

*Sari Grandstaff*
*Woodstock, New York*

away
from the camp
firefly dance

*Sherry Grant*
*Auckland, New Zealand*


first touch
fusion of energy
love is born

*Margaret Anne Gratton*
*Canby, Oregon*


a familiar pin
on the map app
butterflies

*David Grayson*
*Alameda, California*

street litter
the calico kitten
with thick mascara

*John S Green*
*Amman, Jordan*


plant pollen—
appearing as fairy dust
on the garden gnome

*Steven Greene*
*Haddon Township, New Jersey*


can't sleep
one bird is louder
than a city street

*Paula Yardley Griffin*
*Sarasota, Florida*

heartland
deep furrows in
the farmer's brow

*Dana Grover*
*San Jose, California*


dense fog
disembodied voices
walk the street

*Larry Gust*
*Lakeville, Minnesota*


emergency room
man clings to a
battered teddy bear

*Margie Gustafson*
*Lombard, Illinois*

dandelions blooming
on a cool, gray day
sunspots

    *Shir Haberman*
    *Hampton, New Hampshire*

    in her own time
    she opens up
    amaryllis

        *Maureen Lanagan Haggerty*
        *Madison, New Jersey*

this become
  this be change
    this be none

      *Tom Hahney*
      *Bellingham, Washington*

gathering blue
a eulogy delivered
by caesarean

    *Jennifer Hambrick*
    *Worthington, Ohio*


news of his passing
the snow prints
erased

    *John J. Han*
    *Manchester, Missouri*


The silent ballpark,
Three egrets in the outfield,
All set for the fall.

    *Cliff Harbour*
    *Sacramento, California*

dead swan
the light
of a new moon

*Jon Hare*
*Falmouth, Massachusetts*

sakura sakura
followed by
sake sake

*Charles Harmon*
*Whittier, California*

end of autumn
    homesick for someplace
i've never been

*Lev Hart*
*Calgary, Alberta, Canada*

cloud castles
the little girl practices
her curtsy

    *Michele L. Harvey*
    *Hamilton, New York*


black and white penguins    make the list

    *Patricia Harvey*
    *East Longmeadow, Massachusetts*


the light in her eyes candlelit dinner

    *Quamrul Hassan*
    *Fayetteville, Arkansas*

wind twisted trunk
an evergreen
bows to us

   *Shasta Hatter*
   *Gresham, Oregon*




   filtered sunlight
   in the morning forest . . .
   wavy moss

     *Akihiko Hayashi*
     *Osaka, Japan*




     chasing the sun
     over hundreds of miles
     and finding it   gone

       *Elizabeth Hazen*
       *Williston, Vermont*

wild violets
the spell
cast by a weed

*Betsy Hearne*
*Urbana, Illinois*

kneading the dough
I notice
grandmother's knuckles

*Karin Hedetniemi*
*Victoria, Canada*

wildflowers . . .
the meadow whorls with
ballet movements

*Deborah Burke Henderson*
*Ashland, Massachusetts*

alone on the beach
she befriends
a stranded kelp

*Paul Hendricks*
*Missoula, Montana*

where the river bends
two old men stand backlit
in a wooden boat

*chad henry*
*Aurora, Colorado*

wisp of moon
tucks herself in
nighttime secrets

*Nancy Henson*
*Albuquerque, New Mexico*

deep spring
his worn hands build
her dollhouse

*Randall Herman*
*Victoria, Texas*

at my mom's deathbed
we turn to watch a rain cloud
till the pane is wet

*Frank Higgins*
*Kansas City, Missouri*

restless footsteps
evening fog
streaks the window

*Merle Hinchee*
*Cary, North Carolina*

spring comes first
to her plum tree
in Deuteronomy

    *Robert Hirschfield*
    *New York, New York*


gulls
can go
anywhere

    *Judith Hishikawa*
    *Astoria, New York*


Polaroids
still waiting
for clarity

    *Mark Hitri*
    *Fort Worth, Texas*

hauling
the tide
horseshoe crabs

*Jeff Hoagland*
*Hopewell, New Jersey*

crimson light
through the haze
of Canadian wildfires

*Haley Hodge*
*Dover, New Hampshire*

A gentle plink plink.
Steady downpour. This drumbeat
Lulls us, motherly

*Marta Alaina Holliday*
*Hope Hull, Alabama*

stick
by stick
the eagle's nest

*Ruth Holzer*
*Herndon, Virginia*


the chimney's shadow
reaches the forsythia
wine o'clock

*Frank Hooven*
*Morrisville, Pennsylvania*


hummingbird
so much motion in my
one window-wide world

*Christine Horner*
*Walnut Creek, California*

old age
rain fitting into
a slow drip

*Gary Hotham*
*Scaggsville, Maryland*

flying through the night
and into my dreams
trumpeter swans

*Beth Howard*
*Cheyenne, Wyoming*

black eyed susan
total solar eclipse
mirror image

*cp howes*
*Green Bay, Wisconsin*

ushered to the front
at my friend's memorial
I recall his life

*Jennifer Howse*
*Cold Spring, New York*


darker earlier
where clouds diminish
a deeper pink

*Marshall Hryciuk*
*Toronto, Canada*


morning star
always knowing
how old you would be

*Edward Cody Huddleston*
*Baxley, Georgia*

whippoorwills
courtship calls
all night rave

*JL Huffman*
*Blue Ridge Mountains, North Carolina*




airplane door
blows off
corporate dysfunction

*David Q. Hutcheson-Tipton*
*Centennial, Colorado*




midday heat
the jogger's perfume
blocks the berry scent

*Connie Hutchison*
*Kirkland, Washington*

wind comes off the desert
deciding
where to scatter the ashes

    *Gil Jackofsky*
    *San Marcos, California*


rolling thunder—
American muscle cars
flex their engines

    *Rick Jackofsky*
    *Rocky Point, New York*


giving me
the cold shoulder
windchill

    *Roberta Beach Jacobson*
    *Indianola, Iowa*

war-torn country
coaxing a smile
from a child

*Lynne Jambor*
*Vancouver, Canada*

frozen butter the sun in winter

*Peter Jastermsky*
*Yucca Valley, California*

rock garden
embedded in the rock
ancient lichen

*Hans Jongman*
*Welland, Ontario, Canada*

twilight
Joshua trees fade
to silhouette

*Carol Judkins*
*Carlsbad, California*


oil painter clouds an untitled sky

*petro c. k.*
*Seattle, Washington*


*wash me*
on the car window
ragweed morning

*Donna Kaplan*
*Concord, Massachusetts*

angry words
the pine tree untouched
from light and shadow

> *Deborah Karl-Brandt*
> *Bonn, Germany*

peppermint blossoms
sway with dawn breezes and dip
with the weight of bees

> *Robert K Keim*
> *(no location given)*

the daffodils dying
giving birth
to summer

> *Henry Kellogg*
> *Underhill, Vermont*

a shiver of breeze
silver shards of willow
twist the summer light

> *David J Kelly*
> *Dublin, Ireland*




he says it's good
for beating eggs—
Civil War silver

> *Julie Bloss Kelsey*
> *Germantown, Maryland*




old willow basket
full of just picked peaches,
cheeky side up

> *Mary Kendall*
> *Chapel Hill, North Carolina*

A western tanager
grabs my breath
and is gone

    *Philip Kenney*
    *Portland, Oregon*


blistering summer sand
i hopscotch
to my towel

    *Jill Kessler*
    *Bluffton, South Carolina*


middle of the woods
withered old fencepost
without a fence

    *Michael Ketchek*
    *Rochester, New York*

not watching
the total solar eclipse
in bed with Covid

*Howard Lee Kilby*
*Hot Springs, Arkansas*

snowcap mountain peaks
glimpse behind the trees
sunset

*Roy Kindelberger*
*Edmonds, Washington*

quiet unfolds
inside closed elm buds
deep knowing

*Terranda King*
*Albuquerque, New Mexico*

low tide
a hermit crab
upgrades

*Ravi Kiran*
*Hyderabad, India*


geese soar
with my thoughts
i sit

*Michael Kitchen*
*Chesterfield, Michigan*


prancing pink poodle
the German Shepherd
looks away

*kjmunro*
*Whitehorse, Canada*

Cardinals
Birds of
Pray

*Ed Kosiewicz*
*Bradenton, Florida*


94th birthday
more candles
than cake

*Henry W. Kreuter*
*Lebanon, New Jersey*


halide lit field
looking for my pitch
within the fog

*Seth Kronick*
*Whittier, California*

split sunset
the shadow
cast by grief

> *Kimberly Kuchar*
> *Austin, Texas*

dream departs the sound of a downpour

> *Paul Kulwatno*
> *Falls Church, Virginia*

every place
i feel at home . . .
lilacs

> *Jill Lange*
> *Cleveland Heights, Ohio*

a cricket chirps—
quick twitches
of cat whiskers

*Chris Langer*
*Stephenville, Texas*


all the brain cells
I murdered
no headstones

*David G. Lanoue*
*Lexington, Kentucky*


awakening
the yellow noise
of forsythia

*Jim Laurila*
*Florence, Massachusetts*

saying grace—
the little girl
bursts into song

    *Suzanne Leaf-Brock*
    *Ames, Iowa*

Valentine's Day
braving a wind chill factor
of minus one

    *Michael Henry Lee*
    *Saint Augustine, Florida*

dragons sleep
bellies exposed
lichen scaling age-old stone

    *Susannah Lee*
    *Atlanta, Georgia*

Quiet tenderness
Mossy forest eyes conceal
Past unspoken wounds

*Venessa Y. Lee-Estevez*
*Miami, Florida*

unexpected snow
a toddler carries
his sand shovel

*Brenda Lempp*
*Madison, Wisconsin*

Trees erase neighbors
Early leaves not fast enough
Every move is seen

*Edward Lent*
*Guilford, Connecticut*

the sundress strap
slips off her shoulder
koi moon

*Rachel Lentz*
*Colorado Springs, Colorado*


taking a tumble
the child in me
running home

*Barrie Levine*
*Wenham, Massachusetts*


no-fishing sign—
the kingfisher ruffles
its feathers

*Antoinette Libro*
*St. Augustine, Florida*

prepared to lose
her heart again . . .
unborn herons

*Kathryn Liebowitz*
*Groton, Massachusetts*



autumn sunset
a backroad billboard asks
heaven or hell

*Kristen Lindquist*
*Camden, Maine*



morning coffee darkened
the way a colleague mimics
my English

*Chen-ou Liu*
*Ajax, Canada*

winter solstice
the slow drip
from an icicle

*Cyndi Lloyd*
*Riverton, Utah*


purple duct tape
my granddaughter says
my cane is cool

*Renee Londner*
*Prospect, Connecticut*


autumn shadows
i pass the age
dad never reached

*Gregory Longenecker*
*Pasadena, California*

Lake Superior agate
hiding in plain sight
her eyes

*Ellen Lord*
*Charlevoix, Michigan*

rain's end
an iris tongue
slurps the sun

*Amy Losak*
*Teaneck, New Jersey*

GPS
providing an alternate route—
in vitro fertilization

*Kendall Lott*
*Bloomington, Indiana*

gossamer wings
fanning the air
blue dragonfly

*Linda L. Ludwig*
*Inverness, Florida*

the flash
of a parrot's wing
afternoon sun

*Heather Lurie*
*Eyrewell Forest, New Zealand*

our last date—
rain on the lake
ripples on ripples

*Anthony Lusardi*
*Rockaway, New Jersey*

blizzard
still facing each other
a pair of beach chairs

*Doris Jean Lynch*
*Bloomington, Indiana*

sky ribbons flutter
I inhale
aurora borealis

*Jone Rush MacCulloch*
*Happy Valley, Oregon*

New Year's Day
the sea a sea of
white caps

*Patricia J. Machmiller*
*San Jose, California*

again the rain
my stack of unread books
dwindling

 *Kate MacQueen*
 *Chapel Hill, North Carolina*


city park stars blanket the homeless

 *Carole MacRury*
 *Point Roberts, Washington*


silent meditation
the clock echoes
my heartbeat

 *Lillian Nakamura Maguire*
 *Whitehorse, Yukon Canada*

Be edge dwellers
Slowly changing the center.
Be mystics, prophets, poets.

*J. Patrick Mahon*
*Weaverville, North Carolina*

morning rain
blurring the redwoods
his three-note yawn

*Annette Makino*
*Arcata, California*

old friends
making up for lost time—
empty teacups

*Alice Mallory*
*Ashland, Oregon*

above the falls—
the young couple
in everyone's photos

*C.R. Manley*
*Bellevue, Washington*

a broken home
the house finch
builds her nest

*Shirley Marc*
*Springfield, Oregon*

elementary backstroke
with each breath
a glance of sky

*Jeannie Martin*
*Newton, Massachusetts*

unspoken words
a mosquito hawk
hovers at my window

*Seretta Martin*
*San Diego, California*

the stars calling me homesick

*Sharon Martina*
*Warrenville, Illinois*

Born silhouettes
a dorm room
turned into murals

*Jasper Marynczak*
*Albany, New York*

gently grooming
tussled seagrass
rising tide

*Richard L. Matta*
*San Diego, California*


Silent snowfall

Interrupted
Distant shovel scrapes

*Kathleen McAllen*
*Lancaster, Pennsylvania*


the ocean
collecting
every shade of blue

*Mary McCormack*
*La Grange Park, Illinois*

forsythia—
gleaming between stalks
a black cat's eye

*Vicki McCullough*
*Vancouver, Canada*

sidewalk penny—
she rescues
the stranded worm

*Tanya McDonald*
*Happy Valley, Oregon*

the fairy
responsible for my missing socks
strikes again

*Janet McKeehan-Medina*
*Larchmont, New York*

spring rain
patches of green
on the pitch

*Robert B McNeill*
*Winchester, Virginia*


last leaf on the tree
never guessing
it would be me

*MJ Mello*
*Carolina, Rhode Island*


crow by crow the corn wagon's rattle

*Sarah E. Metzler*
*Marion Center, Pennsylvania*

north wind
rivers of white sand
flowing into the sea

*Benjamin T. Miller*
*Carrboro, North Carolina*

his death poem
about quantum physics
warm sakura wind

*Atsuko Mine*
*Matsumoto, Japan*

autumn deepening
her seat in the classroom
still empty

*Matthew Moffett*
*Mt. Pleasant, Michigan*

***Psychosis***
‖: a basketball dribbles :‖
***fff***

*Kati Mohr*
*Nürnberg, Germany*

desolate playground
*ashes ashes*
*we all fall down*

*Beverly Acuff Momoi*
*Mountain View, California*

day after eclipse
sun and clouds romp
to a purple dawn

*Jennifer H. Monaghan*
*Grant, Florida*

New Year's morning
one storm-tossed seagull
above the grey sea

*Ross Moore*
*Belfast, Ireland*


gnawing on dried old peaches how long it's been since we last had sex

*Isabella Mori*
*Vancouver, Canada*


all black keys
this song
made of wind

*Anne Morrigan*
*Ontario, Canada*

stubble field
the scarecrow and i
unemployed

*Kenneth Mory*
*San Jose, Costa Rica*

a warm wind
through the garden
wanderer butterfly

*Leanne Mumford*
*Sydney, Australia*

Island Sanctuary
Giants, strong, guarding, mute, calm
Life within abounds

*Linda Nash*
*Issaquah, Washington*

I am drunk with love,
and I refuse to sober.
Rain, pink petals, rain!

*Anna Andreeva Naydenova*
*Peachtree City, Georgia*



playing hide and seek
in the sky
blue butterflies

*Ross Neher*
*New York, New York*



white picket fence
holding back the ragweed
first tomatoes

*Melissa Leaf Nelson*
*Madison, Wisconsin*

birdsong
setting the tone
spa day

*Stephanie Newbern*
*Bossier City, Louisiana*



tethered
zipline
primal scream

*Renie Newlon*
*Albuquerque, New Mexico*



light—
a particle surfing
its own wave

*Suzanne Niedzielska*
*Glastonbury, Connecticut*

spring winds
trees
find their voice

    *Gareth Nurden*
    *Cwmbran, Wales*

    a bracing wind—
    still the old headstones
    stand unmoved

        *Sean O'Connor*
        *Tipperary, Ireland*

    tomorrow's orals
    another round
    at the bar

        *Karen O'Leary*
        *West Fargo, North Dakota*

memory care
an orange
pierced with cloves

*William O'Sullivan*
*Silver Spring, Maryland*


drone pilot
the crosshairs touch
a man on a bike

*David Oates*
*Athens, Georgia*


chaparral
the surround-sound
of song sparrows

*Helen Ogden*
*Pacific Grove, California*

snow on daffodils
she ignores the freeze warnings
brave enough to smile

*Ashlyn McKayla Ohm*
*Lonsdale, Arkansas*

each month
writes its own poems
almost February

*Ellen Grace Olinger*
*Oostburg, Wisconsin*

people-watching
at the bird sanctuary
fall migration

*Robert A. Oliveira*
*Bonita Springs, Florida*

our young son
at the upstairs window
sunflowers

> *Ben Oliver*
> *Stroud, England*

remembering
spring's first leaves
fiery maple

> *Nancy Orr*
> *Lewiston, Maine*

year of the dragon
an extra red envelope
for the new cat

> *Derek Harootune Otis*
> *Atlanta, Georgia*

in the midst
of downloading my day
two foxes

> *Renée Owen*
> *Sebastopol, California*

fern frost
in the picture window
a family supper

> *Roland Packer*
> *Hamilton, Ontario, Canada*

one more bedtime story—
we tuck her in
to dust

> *Lorraine A Padden*
> *San Diego, California*

stop-motion
among the cattails
a bittern

> *Tom Painting*
> *Atlanta, Georgia*

after the last note
the conductor holds the silence
in his fingertips

> *Robin Palley*
> *Philadelphia, Pennsylvania*

Easter lilies
their natural bloom
on Mother's Day

> *Christa Pandey*
> *Austin, Texas*

peg in the shed—
the salty sweat stains
on dad's gardening hat

*Linda Papanicolaou*
*Palo Alto, California*

autumn sunset
Monarchs meet for
one last dance

*Sarah Paris*
*Santa Rosa, California*

Frost yields to sunlight,
orbs of dew slip silently
from leaves still frozen

*Doug Parkin*
*Salt Lake City, Utah*

daybreak on silky web
spider catches sunrise

*Constance Patrick*
*Sedona, Arizona*

artist pencils the grayscale of his sadness

*Marianne Paul*
*Kitchener, Canada*

as the world grows more insane forsythia

*James A. Paulson*
*Narberth, Pennsylvania*

Bee buzzes weightless
Within a golden chalice—
Sweet poppy café

    *Lynnea Paxton-Honn*
    *Sutter Creek, California*



Combing the beach
Seeking heart-shaped rocks
Signs from Mom

    *Sandra Payne*
    *Studio City, California*



the lake invites me
to write poetry
on its ripples

    *James Penha*
    *Bali, Indonesia*

compass
protractor
drawing out a life

*Ann M. Penton*
*Green Valley, Arizona*

blue eggs
nestled in the nest
sweet pea tendrils rise

*Marjorie Pezzoli*
*San Diego, California*

near the broken wall
of an ancient building grows
a small red tulip

*Margaret Pfeffer*
*Minneapolis, Minnesota*

suburban road
the shriek of a cockatoo
streams past

*Madhuri Pillai*
*Melbourne, Australia*



nobody told me
flowers grew where the dead slept
the war was over

*Scott J. Poole*
*Diablo, California*



at the diner
two old men talk fishing
poached eggs

*Suzanne Powell*
*Ottawa, Canada*

stained glass window
a swallow flies
across the night sky

*Vanessa Proctor*
*Sydney, Australia*


lambing season
the ewes eye my belly
expectantly

*m. shane pruett*
*Salem, Oregon*


floating on
the tranquil stream
rubber duck

*Kathryn Pumphrey*
*Lynchburg, Virginia*

Yahtzee!
5 of a kind
at the kitchen table

*Diane Puterbaugh*
*Jackson, Tennessee*

    bouncing tourist boats
    off the coast of Ceylon
    blue whales wave . . .

    *Veeraja R*
    *Franklin, Tennessee*

    bright yellow
    at spring sunrise
    daffodils

        *Barth H. Ragatz*
        *Fort Wayne, Indiana*

rising through clouds
from early morning dreams
two black swans

*Katherine Raine*
*Cromwell, New Zealand*

empty glasses
we polish off
our stories

*Holli Rainwater*
*Fresno, Ohio*

sax glissando
whiskey over
ice cubes

*j rap*
*Albuquerque, New Mexico*

Beak upward to sky
Stale fries, Walmart parking lot
Manna from heaven

*Annette Reasoner*
*Shallowater, Texas*


the present
haunted by the past
empty bottle

*Addison Redley*
*London, United Kingdom*


singing in public
a blue morpho
opens its wings

*Dian Duchin Reed*
*Soquel, California*

wanting to take back
so many words
tide's ebb

> *Dave Reynolds*
> *Colorado Springs, Colorado*

brown burrs
stuck to my socks
nosey neighbors

> *Sharon Rhutasel-Jones*
> *Los Ranchos, New Mexico*

a burst of crocus
each abuzz
with its own bee

> *Gail Ribeck*
> *Rockport, Maine*

dandelion seeds
this breeze, too
setting me free

*Bryan Rickert*
*Belleville, Illinois*

child's cowboy hat
on a high shelf
so much not done

*Edward J. Rielly*
*Westbrook, Maine*

spring stroll
jacarandas in bloom
and "Purple Rain" on repeat

*Julie Riggott*
*Glendale, California*

midday sun
a gardener weeding
his shadow

    *Karen Rizzo*
    *Warwick, Rhode Island*


the butterfly stops and starts the stalking cat

    *Joseph Robello*
    *Mill Valley, California*


early spring—
    songs crescendo
into squawks

    *Susan Lee Roberts*
    *Montesano, Washington*

this hill
driving my car
into the sun

    *Barbara Robinette*
    *Viola, Arkansas*


herders staggered
along the horizon
evening stars

    *Chad Lee Robinson*
    *Pierre, South Dakota*


bargaining stage
chrysanthemum buds
still sepal-tight

    *Michele Root-Bernstein*
    *East Lansing, Michigan*

Belly filled with lives
a stray cat readies as she
builds a bed of straw

*Lorraine Rose*
*Brewster, New York*

rain-streaked windows
how to ease
her sadness?

*Ce Rosenow*
*Eugene, Oregon*

before dawn
the full moon sets
smiling

*Joan W Rossi*
*Haverhill, Massachusetts*

forgetting myself
clouds disperse
in the summer breeze

>　*Nicholas H. Rossler*
>　*Arvada, Colorado*

from the oven
the smell of bread
open house

>　*Raymond C Roy*
>　*Winston-Salem, North Carolina*

we discuss
the price we paid . . .
Indian mangoes

>　*Suraja Menon Roychowdhury*
>　*Lexington, Massachusetts*

my neighbor
begins another story
the undersong of crickets

*Maggie Roycraft*
*Morristown, New Jersey*



ancient oak
in his shadow
mine

*Lidia Rozmus*
*Kraków, Poland*



my sister's
final chemo round
first peach blossom

*Janet Ruth*
*Corrales, New Mexico*

shuffling through dry leaves
crackle
old joints

*Ellen Ryan*
*Lone Tree, Colorado*




hometown road
the sea snail's
muscled foot

*Barbara Sabol*
*Akron, Ohio*




cloudy day
the snowfield melts
into the sky

*Marianne Sahlin*
*Gothenburg, Sweden*

a single word
re-ignites the fire
Chinook wind

*Jacob D. Salzer*
*Vancouver, Washington*


dawn through
the eyelet curtain
lucid dreaming

*Kelly Sargent*
*Williston, Vermont*


stopping
at every rabbit hole
bobcat tracks

*Cam M. Sato*
*Williston, Vermont*

holes in the clouds
a cool breeze carries
sirens

*Agnes Eva Savich*
*Austin, Texas*



outdoor cafe
cherry blossoms garnish
my gin and tonic

*Barbara Tate Sayre*
*Winchester, Tennessee*



all day rain
undiluted
dogwood blossoms

*Michelle Schaefer*
*Bothell, Washington*

range cattle burnish
the watering hole snag . . .
 autumn deepens

*Judith Morrison Schallberger
San Jose, California*

butterfly
gone on a breeze
her late spirit

*Joseph N. Schmidt Jr.
Alameda, California*

subliminal crickets the ash of stars

*Ann K. Schwader
Westminster, Colorado*

speaking of stem cells
lion tails
in the prairie grass

*Dan Schwerin*
*Sun Prairie, Wisconsin*


larches
playing possum . . .
winter's end

*Julie Schwerin*
*Sun Prairie, Wisconsin*


sunlight
the splash fades
from a river stone

*Paula Sears*
*Exeter, New Hampshire*

fresh snow melting
under bright sun—
April strawberries

*Elizabeth Shack*
*Urbana, Illinois*


a new wobble
in my walk
acorns on the trail

*Adelaide B. Shaw*
*Somers, New York*


bud break
wild plums
heralding spring

*Michael Sheffield*
*Sonoma Valley, California*

on butterfly wings of the blue rock thrush

*Charlie Shiotani*
*Watsonville, California*

dementia
his life a series
of vignettes

*Tomislav Sjekloća*
*Cetinje, Montenegro*

contrail
from Orion's bow
Valentine's Day

*George Skane*
*Georgetown, Massachusetts*

drizzle tapers
more missiles rain
down on children

*Crystal Simone Smith*
*Durham, North Carolina*

bluebird luncheon
sweet berries served
on pokeweed branches

*Danna Smith*
*Woodbridge, California*

birdsong
pushes the storm clouds
to distant mountains

*Lyle Smith*
*West Sacramento, California*

No. 2 pencil
Bubbling in answers
To life's questions

*Michael K Smith*
*Knoxville, Tennessee*


winter snowfall
skeletal trees
alive in white

*Thomas Smith*
*Austin, Texas*


My dog parts
the swamp grass
with her muzzle

*Bill Smoot*
*Berkeley, California*

question mark butterfly
Google images
says so

*Matt Snyder*
*Pittsboro, North Carolina*


dawn chorus—
the chitter-chatter
of my thoughts

*Sheila Sondik*
*Bellingham, Washington*


the buzz about
camping in The Florida Keys—
mosquitoes

*Lisa Sparaco*
*Pearland, Texas*

smashed crabapples
on the sidewalk
school opens

*Jill Spealman*
*Glen Ellyn, Illinois*

cleaning up
in the backyard
meteor shower

*Evan Spivack*
*Teaneck, New Jersey*

first cut of the lawn
my garden-shed spider
along for the ride

*susan spooner*
*Victoria, Canada*

prairie's hum
along a chorus of cicadas
my tinnitus

*Sandra St-Laurent*
*Whitehorse, Canada*

moonless night—
she borrows
my dream-catcher

*Bonnie Stepenoff*
*Chesterfield, Missouri*

three cabbage whites
flutter energetically
day one or day ten?

*Marsha Stern*
*Bellows Falls, Vermont*

slow news day
robins fight over borders
only they can see

> *Dylan Stover*
> *Cuyahoga Falls, Ohio*

asperitas
my shape changing
with the wind

> *Debbie Strange*
> *Winnipeg, Canada*

New Year's Day
wondering if hangover
is a season word

> *Lee Strong*
> *Rochester, New York*

winter walk . . .
a golden retriever
wagging the sun

*Ann Sullivan*
*Arlington, Massachusetts*


leaky pipes
the plumber sings an aria
from under the sink

*Dennis Sullivan*
*Arcata, California*


gunshy the blue excluded by Picasso

*Alan Summers*
*Chippenham, England*

manicured lawn—
an uprising
of buttercups

*Dean Summers*
*Renton, Washington*


hummingbirds return
to my plastic flowers—
afternoon sun

*Laurance Sumners*
*Lufkin, Texas*


the nomadic life
of wild orchids
falling stars

*Eric Sundquist*
*Batesville, Virginia*

fresh green leaves
shadowing on a street piano
May is still dazzling for me

*Ryoko M. Suzuki*
*Otsu, Japan*

wiping his nose print
from the passenger side window
one last time

*R. J. Swanson*
*Rollingbay, Washington*

windy day
hearing the ocean
without the shell

*Carol Tagstrom*
*Littleton, Colorado*

circus of my mind
taming the wild tigers
without a whip

*Louann Talbert*
*Napa, California*


a dandelion wishing for more of the same

*Rick Tarquinio*
*Woodruff, New Jersey*


pine warbler
the welcoming rhythm
of dinner for one

*Margaret Tau*
*New Bern, North Carolina*

elf on a shelf
the secrets
he must know

*Leon Tefft*
*Greenville, South Carolina*


bone scan
the density
of Earthshine

*Angela Terry*
*Sequim, Washington*


road stand seed packet
nothing comes up
as planned

*Jennifer Thiermann*
*Glenview, Illinois*

cutting through the kelp
a fisherman bleeds
an ocean

*R.C. Thomas*
*Plymouth, United Kingdom*

cross necklace
faith sways from
the rearview mirror

*Ken Thompson*
*Tuckahoe, New Jersey*

school crossing guard
stops traffic
for pensioners

*Linda Thompson*
*Colorado Springs, Colorado*

Fond memories
my mother
no longer remembers

*Terri. A. Thorfinnson*
*West Sacramento, California*

longest day
filling an old pine
a cacophony of grackles

*Carly Siegel Thorp*
*Sterling, Massachusetts*

lazy day . . .
wrapped around my finger
line to the bobber

*Richard Tice*
*Kent, Washington*

in the hello
from our mailman
a subdued delivery

> Nathanael Tico
> San Francisco, California

locking eyes
with the dragon
—a shift in the wind

> Corine Timmer
> Faro, Portugal

Droplets on my windowsill
Racing toward the finish line
Tears on a cold rainy day

> Hope Tomko
> Highland Park, New Jersey

breaking cloud
she dips her brush
in azure

*Xenia Tran*
*Nairn, Scotland*

first in line
for the Jackson Pollock show
Dexter Morgan

*Charles Trumbull*
*Santa Fe, New Mexico*

your white truck
will never pull in again
cherry petal rain

*Barbara Ungar*
*Saratoga Springs, New York*
*in honor of Stuart Bartow*

bare spruce
overcome with lichen
another shade of green

*Andrea Vlahakis*
*Woodbury, Connecticut*

Exiting the rainforest
her face splashed
with sun

*Richard H Wagner*
*Tucson, Arizona*

end of the salmon run
a canopy of stars so bright
it could be a tall tale

*Patricia Wakimoto*
*Gardena, California*

second hand in the margins second story

*Margaret Walker*
*Lincoln, Nebraska*


the clink
of wine in the car trunk
autumn aspens

*Marilyn Walker*
*Madison, Georgia*


blood moon more brilliant as it pales

*Diane Wallihan*
*Port Townsend, Washington*

somewhere in Kansas
staring at the universe
a scarecrow

*Jeffery Walthall*
*Fairfax, Virginia*

small craft advisory
a Viagra pop-up
on the radar

*Lew Watts*
*Chicago, Illinois*

infield fly—
the chatter of starlings
circling shortstop

*Joseph P. Wechselberger*
*Browns Mills, New Jersey*

moonless night
fog creeps across
the empty pond

*Adèle Weers*
*Zurich, Switzerland*

windblown leaves
the beauty
rearranged

*Mary Weidensaul*
*Granby, Massachusetts*

clouds dot
her 'i's . . .
gran's pie recipe

*Linda Weir*
*Ellicott City, Maryland*

beauty is truth
the beached whale
sinking into sand

*Michael Dylan Welch*
*Sammamish, Washington*




morning chill
the pause between
steeping and sipping

*Christine Wenk-Harrison*
*Lago Vista, Texas*




dusk at midday the hope held in birdsong

*Marcie Wessels*
*San Diego, California*

calling cardinal
on a snow-covered branch
red maple buds

*Stephanie Wharton*
*Parkesburg, Pennsylvania*

pride weekend over
a woman in a work truck
brushes out her wig

*Allyson Whipple*
*St. Louis, Missouri*

Lured by tinkling bells
Sprinkle tops and waffle cones
Children get ice cream.

*Bruce E. Whitacre*
*Forest Hills, New York*

tailor's chalk ~
his perfectly curved
lines

*Robin White*
*Deerfield, New Hampshire*

border crossing the lives we abandon

*Scott Wiggerman*
*Albuquerque, New Mexico*

evening meditation . . .
the hours melt into
pastels

*Laurie Wilcox-Meyer*
*Asheville, North Carolina*

bossa nova
rose hips swaying
in a gentle breeze

*Tony Williams*
*Scotland*

early autumn—
a breeze re-rains the rain
through the maples

*Billie Wilson*
*Juneau, Alaska*

leaving for China
the orchid we buy
to welcome us home

*Kathabela Wilson*
*Pasadena, California*

hidden pond
giving you my pebble
to skip

*Jamie Wimberly*
*Alpharetta, Georgia*


old family videos
a younger you winks
at me

*Valorie Broadhurst Woerdehoff*
*Dubuque, Iowa*


Mosquito hawks fly
Low under the cedar tree
stepping into spring

*Jackie Wolven*
*Eureka Springs, Arkansas*

the tiniest buds
on the riverside bushes
snowing

*Kathryn Wood*
*Bend, Oregon*


river of stars
baby's eyes in dreamland
flickering

*Alison Woolpert*
*Santa Cruz, California*


spring yard sale
the young widow lays out
his winter clothes

*Jay Wright*
*Anderson, South Carolina*

hazy moon
a toe in three oceans
at Kanyakumari

*Susan Yavaniski*
*Cohoes, New York*

partly risen dough
half of me resists
growing up

*Nitu Yumnam*
*West Bengal, India*

winter morning—
the chimney's shadow
glitters white

*Sherry Zhou*
*Rochester, Minnesota*

forgiving the sun
as it sinks beyond the sea
hospice watch

*J. Zimmerman*
*Santa Cruz, California*

little mosquito
go away! I'm practicing
non-separation

*Lynda Zwinger*
*Tucson, Arizona*

# Index of Poets

| | | | |
|---|---|---|---|
| Ackroyd, Meredith | 7 | Berglund, Jerome | 20 |
| Adams, Elaine Parker | 7 | Berkley, John | 20 |
| Ahern, Mimi | 8 | Bhusal, Shiva | 20 |
| Aiello, Dennise | 8 | Bisshie | 21 |
| Allyson, Jessica | 8 | Black, Elizabeth | 21 |
| Anand, Rupa | 9 | Blair, Shawn | 21 |
| Anderson, Barbara Mosbacher | 9 | Blocker, Jack | 22 |
| Anderson, Cynthia | 9 | Blood, Shannon M. | 22 |
| Angyal, Jenny Ward | 10 | Blumner, Jacob | 22 |
| Anne, Lois | 10 | Board, Mykel | 23 |
| Anstett, Aaron | 10 | Bond, Susan | 23 |
| Aoyagi, Fay | 11 | Borne, Miriam | 23 |
| Arnold, Betty | 11 | Boughton, Andrea | 24 |
| Arthen, Eric | 11 | brady, brett | 24 |
| Asfari, Inas | 12 | Brann, Henry | 24 |
| Ashbaugh, Marilyn | 12 | Brannon, Luke | 25 |
| Ashmore, Kathi | 12 | Brennan, Ashley Charlotte | 25 |
| Ashwell, Joanna | 13 | Brickley, Chuck | 25 |
| Atkins, Marcie Flinchum | 13 | Brooks, Randy | 26 |
| Baatz, Carolyn Marie | 13 | Broscious, S. David | 26 |
| Bahr, Steve | 14 | Brown, Daniel W. | 26 |
| Baird, Don | 14 | Brown, LaMon | 27 |
| Bales, Chandra | 14 | Brown, Roberta | 27 |
| Balistreri, Jo | 15 | Bruce, B. L. | 27 |
| Ballou, Michelle | 15 | Bruner, Chris | 28 |
| Banks, Caroline Giles | 15 | Bruntil, Robert | 28 |
| Banwarth, Francine | 16 | Budan, John | 28 |
| Barksdale, Sheila | 16 | Buettner, Marjorie | 29 |
| Barnes, Peter | 16 | Burgess, Merle | 29 |
| Barzacchini, Mike | 17 | Burke, Alanna C. | 29 |
| Basist, Dyana | 17 | Burridge, Marylyn | 30 |
| Bateman, Sam | 17 | Byrnes, Sondra J. | 30 |
| Beard, Susan K | 18 | Camargo, Claire Vogel | 30 |
| Beary, Roberta | 18 | Campbell, Pris | 31 |
| Becherer, Lori | 18 | Canby, Joan | 31 |
| Bennett, Brad | 19 | Cancro, Theresa A. | 31 |
| Berardi, Bennett | 19 | Caretti, Matthew | 32 |
| Berger, Maxianne | 19 | Carns, Teri White | 32 |

| | | | | |
|---|---|---|---|---|
| Carrier, Ken | 32 | | Davis, Lew | 45 |
| Carrington, Wes | 33 | | Davis, Pat | 45 |
| Carter, R. P. | 33 | | Daw, Danny | 46 |
| Cashman, David | 33 | | Day, Cherie Hunter | 46 |
| Castaldi, Erin | 34 | | Day, Nancy Taylor | 46 |
| Castle, Aidan | 34 | | De Pascuale, Juan Edgardo | 47 |
| Cates, Anna | 34 | | Decker, Kathleen P. | 47 |
| Causey, Paul | 35 | | Dee, Billie | 47 |
| Cheng, Joan | 35 | | DeFatta, Vincent | 48 |
| Cheung, Antoinette | 35 | | Defibaugh, M. R. | 48 |
| Chockley, Thomas | 36 | | DeLong, Jim | 48 |
| Chou, Jackie | 36 | | DePaolo, Rob | 49 |
| Chula, Margaret | 36 | | Dewar, Robert | 49 |
| Church, L. Teresa | 37 | | Diamond, Elliot | 49 |
| Ciarrocchi, John Paul | 37 | | Digregorio, Charlotte | 50 |
| Claire, Joshua St. | 37 | | Dodge, Thomas | 50 |
| Clark, Gordon | 38 | | Dombrosky, Sherri | 50 |
| Clark, Rick | 38 | | Donovan, Fred | 51 |
| Clements, Marcyn Del | 38 | | Doppler, Janice | 51 |
| Coats, Glenn G. | 39 | | Dringenberg, Hans C. | 51 |
| Cobert, Lee | 39 | | Drummy, M F | 52 |
| Cobourne, Wendy | 39 | | Duclos, Aimé E | 52 |
| Colgan, Stephen | 40 | | Dudley, Michael | 52 |
| Colyer, Howard | 40 | | Eberhart, Flora Inez | 53 |
| Conway, Sophia | 40 | | Edge, Lynn | 53 |
| Cook, Bryan D. | 41 | | Eklund-Cheong, Anna | 53 |
| Cook, Wanda | 41 | | Ellis, Jim | 54 |
| Cordeiro, Paul | 41 | | English, Jonathan | 54 |
| Courtney, Sue | 42 | | Epstein, Robert | 54 |
| Cox, Dina E | 42 | | Erlandson, Robert | 55 |
| Cramer, Nichael | 42 | | Ettinger, Eavonka | 55 |
| Cremin, Tim | 43 | | Evans, Judson | 55 |
| Cruz, Alvin B. | 43 | | Evershed, Adele | 56 |
| Cruz, Daniel Shank | 43 | | Evetts, Keith | 56 |
| Cruzan, Patricia | 44 | | Fainzilber, Mike | 56 |
| Curtis, Dan | 44 | | Fanto, Elizabeth | 57 |
| Daneva, Maya | 44 | | Farner, Susan | 57 |
| Davies, Keith | 45 | | Farrar, Mark Stuart | 57 |

| | | | | |
|---|---|---|---|---|
| Farrell, Frances | 58 | Grandstaff, Sari | 70 |
| Farrelly, Colleen M. | 58 | Grant, Sherry | 71 |
| Favret, Jeanne | 58 | Gratton, Margaret Anne | 71 |
| Feehrer, Barbara | 59 | Grayson, David | 71 |
| Feingold, Bruce H. | 59 | Green, John S | 72 |
| Felong, Andy | 59 | Greene, Steven | 72 |
| Fernandez, Nancy Marie | 60 | Griffin, Paula Yardley | 72 |
| Festa, Thomas | 60 | Grover, Dana | 73 |
| Fingon, Joan | 60 | Gust, Larry | 73 |
| Fischer, P. H. | 61 | Gustafson, Margie | 73 |
| Flanagan, Michael | 61 | Haberman, Shir | 74 |
| Fontaine-Pincince, Denise | 61 | Haggerty, Maureen Lanagan | 74 |
| Forges-Ryan, Sylvia | 62 | Hahney, Tom | 74 |
| Forrester, Mark | 62 | Hambrick, Jennifer | 75 |
| Forsythe, Robert | 62 | Han, John J. | 75 |
| Freeman, Jason | 63 | Harbour, Cliff | 75 |
| French, Terri L. | 63 | Hare, Jon | 76 |
| Friedenberg, Jay | 63 | Harmon, Charles | 76 |
| Friedman, Seth | 64 | Hart, Lev | 76 |
| Gaa, Ben | 64 | Harvey, Michele L. | 77 |
| Galasso, William Scott | 64 | Harvey, Patricia | 77 |
| Galko, Michael J. | 65 | Hassan, Quamrul | 77 |
| Gallaher, Cynthia | 65 | Hatter, Shasta | 78 |
| Gallia, Al | 65 | Hayashi, Akihiko | 78 |
| Garcia, Dianne | 66 | Hazen, Elizabeth | 78 |
| Gay, Garry | 66 | Hearne, Betsy | 79 |
| Gehant, Marilyn | 66 | Hedetniemi, Karin | 79 |
| Gentile, Nicholas | 67 | Henderson, Deborah Burke | 79 |
| Gerlits, Lisa | 67 | Hendricks, Paul | 80 |
| Gilli, Ferris | 67 | henry, chad | 80 |
| Gilliland, Robert | 68 | Henson, Nancy | 80 |
| Giorgis, Joette | 68 | Herman, Randall | 81 |
| Godwin, Susan | 68 | Higgins, Frank | 81 |
| Goldbach, Kathy | 69 | Hinchee, Merle | 81 |
| Goodman-Milone, Connie | 69 | Hirschfield, Robert | 82 |
| Gorman, LeRoy | 69 | Hishikawa, Judith | 82 |
| Graham, Adam | 70 | Hitri, Mark | 82 |
| Graham, JC | 70 | Hoagland, Jeff | 83 |

| | | | | |
|---|---|---|---|---|
| Hodge, Haley | 83 | | Kosiewicz, Ed | 96 |
| Holliday, Marta Alaina | 83 | | Kreuter, Henry W. | 96 |
| Holzer, Ruth | 84 | | Kronick, Seth | 96 |
| Hooven, Frank | 84 | | Kuchar, Kimberly | 97 |
| Horner, Christine | 84 | | Kulwatno, Paul | 97 |
| Hotham, Gary | 85 | | Lange, Jill | 97 |
| Howard, Beth | 85 | | Langer, Chris | 98 |
| howes, cp | 85 | | Lanoue, David G. | 98 |
| Howse, Jennifer | 86 | | Laurila, Jim | 98 |
| Hryciuk, Marshall | 86 | | Leaf-Brock, Suzanne | 99 |
| Huddleston, Edward Cody | 86 | | Lee, Michael Henry | 99 |
| Huffman, JL | 87 | | Lee, Susannah | 99 |
| Hutcheson-Tipton, David Q. | 87 | | Lee-Estevez, Venessa Y. | 100 |
| Hutchison, Connie | 87 | | Lempp, Brenda | 100 |
| Jackofsky, Gil | 88 | | Lent, Edward | 100 |
| Jackofsky, Rick | 88 | | Lentz, Rachel | 101 |
| Jacobson, Roberta Beach | 88 | | Levine, Barrie | 101 |
| Jambor, Lynne | 89 | | Libro, Antoinette | 101 |
| Jastermsky, Peter | 89 | | Liebowitz, Kathryn | 102 |
| Jongman, Hans | 89 | | Lindquist, Kristen | 102 |
| Judkins, Carol | 90 | | Liu, Chen-ou | 102 |
| k., petro c. | 90 | | Lloyd, Cyndi | 103 |
| Kaplan, Donna | 90 | | Londner, Renee | 103 |
| Karl-Brandt, Deborah | 91 | | Longenecker, Gregory | 103 |
| Keim, Robert K | 91 | | Lord, Ellen | 104 |
| Kellogg, Henry | 91 | | Losak, Amy | 104 |
| Kelly, David J | 92 | | Lott, Kendall | 104 |
| Kelsey, Julie Bloss | 92 | | Ludwig, Linda L. | 105 |
| Kendall, Mary | 92 | | Lurie, Heather | 105 |
| Kenney, Philip | 93 | | Lusardi, Anthony | 105 |
| Kessler, Jill | 93 | | Lynch, Doris Jean | 106 |
| Ketchek, Michael | 93 | | MacCulloch, Jone Rush | 106 |
| Kilby, Howard Lee | 94 | | Machmiller, Patricia J. | 106 |
| Kindelberger, Roy | 94 | | MacQueen, Kate | 107 |
| King, Terranda | 94 | | MacRury, Carole | 107 |
| Kiran, Ravi | 95 | | Maguire, Lillian Nakamura | 107 |
| Kitchen, Michael | 95 | | Mahon, J. Patrick | 108 |
| kjmunro | 95 | | Makino, Annette | 108 |

| | | | | |
|---|---|---|---|---|
| Mallory, Alice | 108 | Oates, David | 121 |
| Manley, C.R. | 109 | Ogden, Helen | 121 |
| Marc, Shirley | 109 | Ohm, Ashlyn McKayla | 122 |
| Martin, Jeannie | 109 | Olinger, Ellen Grace | 122 |
| Martin, Seretta | 110 | Oliveira, Robert A. | 122 |
| Martina, Sharon | 110 | Oliver, Ben | 123 |
| Marynczak, Jasper | 110 | Orr, Nancy | 123 |
| Matta, Richard L. | 111 | Otis, Derek Harootune | 123 |
| McAllen, Kathleen | 111 | Owen, Renée | 124 |
| McCormack, Mary | 111 | Packer, Roland | 124 |
| McCullough, Vicki | 112 | Padden, Lorraine A | 124 |
| McDonald, Tanya | 112 | Painting, Tom | 125 |
| McKeehan-Medina, Janet | 112 | Palley, Robin | 125 |
| McNeill, Robert B | 113 | Pandey, Christa | 125 |
| Mello, MJ | 113 | Papanicolaou, Linda | 126 |
| Metzler, Sarah E. | 113 | Paris, Sarah | 126 |
| Miller, Benjamin T. | 114 | Parkin, Doug | 126 |
| Mine, Atsuko | 114 | Patrick, Constance | 127 |
| Moffett, Matthew | 114 | Paul, Marianne | 127 |
| Mohr, Kati | 115 | Paulson, James A. | 127 |
| Momoi, Beverly Acuff | 115 | Paxton-Honn, Lynnea | 128 |
| Monaghan, Jennifer H. | 115 | Payne, Sandra | 128 |
| Moore, Ross | 116 | Penha, James | 128 |
| Mori, Isabella | 116 | Penton, Ann M. | 129 |
| Morrigan, Anne | 116 | Pezzoli, Marjorie | 129 |
| Mory, Kenneth | 117 | Pfeffer, Margaret | 129 |
| Mumford, Leanne | 117 | Pillai, Madhuri | 130 |
| Nash, Linda | 117 | Poole, Scott J. | 130 |
| Naydenova, Anna Andreeva | 118 | Powell, Suzanne | 130 |
| Neher, Ross | 118 | Proctor, Vanessa | 131 |
| Nelson, Melissa Leaf | 118 | pruett, m. shane | 131 |
| Newbern, Stephanie | 119 | Pumphrey, Kathryn | 131 |
| Newlon, Renie | 119 | Puterbaugh, Diane | 132 |
| Niedzielska, Suzanne | 119 | R, Veeraja | 132 |
| Nurden, Gareth | 120 | Ragatz, Barth H. | 132 |
| O'Connor, Sean | 120 | Raine, Katherine | 133 |
| O'Leary, Karen | 120 | Rainwater, Holli | 133 |
| O'Sullivan, William | 121 | rap, j | 133 |

| | | | | |
|---|---|---|---|---|
| Reasoner, Annette | 134 | | Sears, Paula | 146 |
| Redley, Addison | 134 | | Shack, Elizabeth | 147 |
| Reed, Dian Duchin | 134 | | Shaw, Adelaide B. | 147 |
| Reynolds, Dave | 135 | | Sheffield, Michael | 147 |
| Rhutasel-Jones, Sharon | 135 | | Shiotani, Charlie | 148 |
| Ribeck, Gail | 135 | | Sjekloća, Tomislav | 148 |
| Rickert, Bryan | 136 | | Skane, George | 148 |
| Rielly, Edward J. | 136 | | Smith, Crystal Simone | 149 |
| Riggott, Julie | 136 | | Smith, Danna | 149 |
| Rizzo, Karen | 137 | | Smith, Lyle | 149 |
| Robello, Joseph | 137 | | Smith, Michael K | 150 |
| Roberts, Susan Lee | 137 | | Smith, Thomas | 150 |
| Robinette, Barbara | 138 | | Smoot, Bill | 150 |
| Robinson, Chad Lee | 138 | | Snyder, Matt | 151 |
| Root-Bernstein, Michele | 138 | | Sondik, Sheila | 151 |
| Rose, Lorraine | 139 | | Sparaco, Lisa | 151 |
| Rosenow, Ce | 139 | | Spealman, Jill | 152 |
| Rossi, Joan W | 139 | | Spivack, Evan | 152 |
| Rossler, Nicholas H. | 140 | | spooner, susan | 152 |
| Roy, Raymond C | 140 | | St-Laurent, Sandra | 153 |
| Roychowdhury, Suraja Menon | 140 | | Stepenoff, Bonnie | 153 |
| Roycraft, Maggie | 141 | | Stern, Marsha | 153 |
| Rozmus, Lidia | 141 | | Stover, Dylan | 154 |
| Ruth, Janet | 141 | | Strange, Debbie | 154 |
| Ryan, Ellen | 142 | | Strong, Lee | 154 |
| Sabol, Barbara | 142 | | Sullivan, Ann | 155 |
| Sahlin, Marianne | 142 | | Sullivan, Dennis | 155 |
| Salzer, Jacob D. | 143 | | Summers, Alan | 155 |
| Sargent, Kelly | 143 | | Summers, Dean | 156 |
| Sato, Cam M. | 143 | | Sumners, Laurance | 156 |
| Savich, Agnes Eva | 144 | | Sundquist, Eric | 156 |
| Sayre, Barbara Tate | 144 | | Suzuki, Ryoko M. | 157 |
| Schaefer, Michelle | 144 | | Swanson, R. J. | 157 |
| Schallberger, Judith Morrison | 145 | | Tagstrom, Carol | 157 |
| Schmidt, Jr., Joseph N. | 145 | | Talbert, Louann | 158 |
| Schwader, Ann K. | 145 | | Tarquinio, Rick | 158 |
| Schwerin, Dan | 146 | | Tau, Margaret | 158 |
| Schwerin, Julie | 146 | | Tefft, Leon | 159 |

| | | | | |
|---|---|---|---|---|
| Terry, Angela | 159 | Weir, Linda | 167 |
| Thiermann, Jennifer | 159 | Welch, Michael Dylan | 168 |
| Thomas, R.C. | 160 | Wenk-Harrison, Christine | 168 |
| Thompson, Ken | 160 | Wessels, Marcie | 168 |
| Thompson, Linda | 160 | Wharton, Stephanie | 169 |
| Thorfinnson, Terri. A. | 161 | Whipple, Allyson | 169 |
| Thorp, Carly Siegel | 161 | Whitacre, Bruce E. | 169 |
| Tice, Richard | 161 | White, Robin | 170 |
| Tico, Nathanael | 162 | Wiggerman, Scott | 170 |
| Timmer, Corine | 162 | Wilcox-Meyer, Laurie | 170 |
| Tomko, Hope | 162 | Williams, Tony | 171 |
| Tran, Xenia | 163 | Wilson, Billie | 171 |
| Trumbull, Charles | 163 | Wilson, Kathabela | 171 |
| Ungar, Barbara | 163 | Wimberly, Jamie | 172 |
| Vlahakis, Andrea | 164 | Woerdehoff, Valorie Broadhurst | 172 |
| Wagner, Richard H | 164 | Wolven, Jackie | 172 |
| Wakimoto, Patricia | 164 | Wood, Kathryn | 173 |
| Walker, Margaret | 165 | Woolpert, Alison | 173 |
| Walker, Marilyn | 165 | Wright, Jay | 173 |
| Wallihan, Diane | 165 | Yavaniski, Susan | 174 |
| Walthall, Jeffery | 166 | Yumnam, Nitu | 174 |
| Watts, Lew | 166 | Zhou, Sherry | 174 |
| Wechselberger, Joseph P. | 166 | Zimmerman, J. | 175 |
| Weers, Adèle | 167 | Zwinger, Lynda | 175 |
| Weidensaul, Mary | 167 | | |